AS I RECALL:
WINGS OF REMEMBRANCE

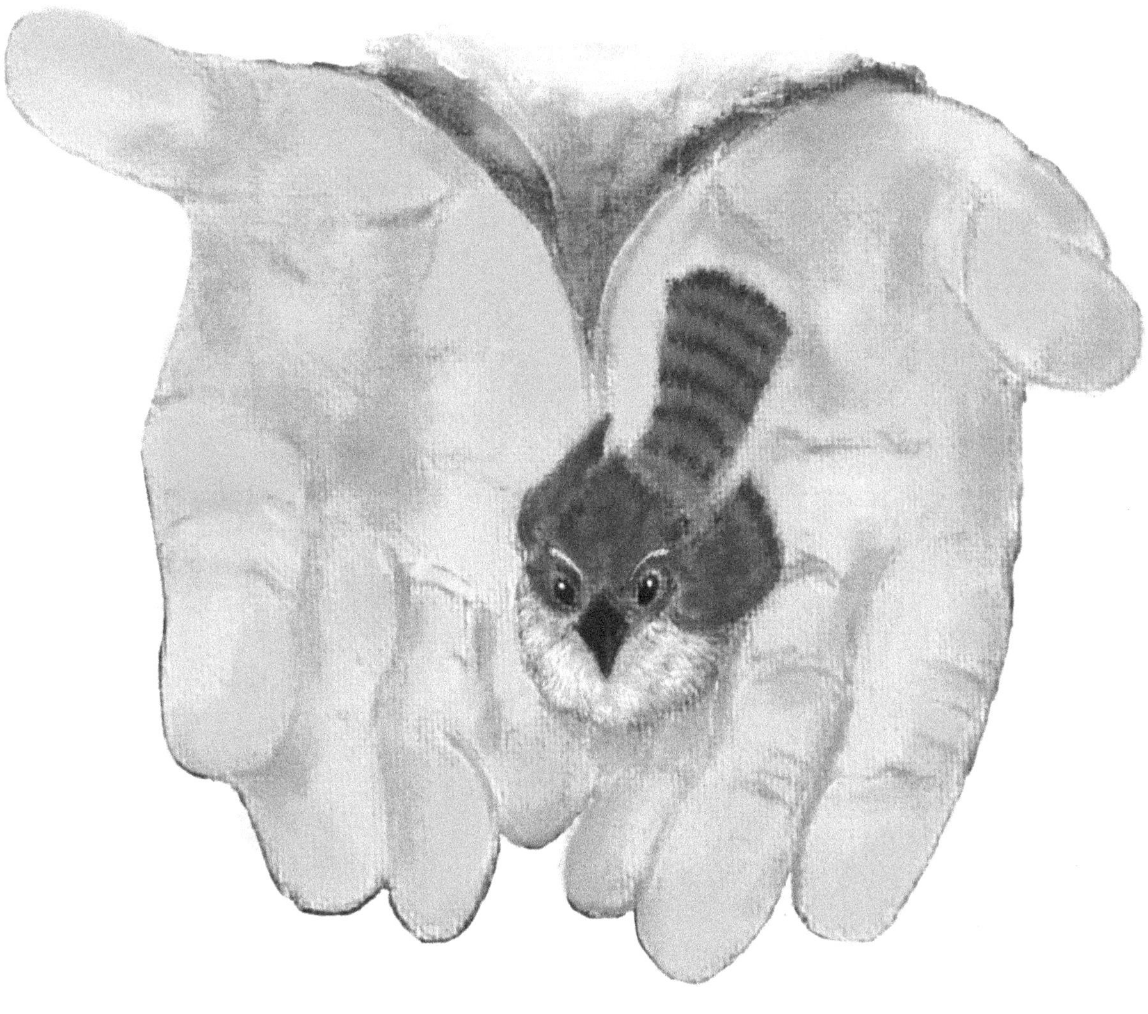

Mark Duffield

Illustrated by Nancy O'Hearn

Strategic Book Publishing and Rights Co.

Strategic Book Publishing and Rights Co., LLC
USA | Singapore
www.sbpra.net

For information about special discounts for bulk purchases, please contact Strategic Book Publishing and Rights Co. Special Sales, at bookorder@sbpra.net.

ISBN: 978-1-68235-724-8

Front and back cover designed by Sharon Duffield

Book Design: Suzanne Kelly

Special thanks to:

Jennifer Hill

Nancy Ullmann

Sandy Giardi

Julia Landwehr

INTRODUCTION

The house wren is a small bird and is considered to be a harbinger of spring. It is said that wrens have special qualities that inspire one to become a better, happier version of ourselves. Our father has always had an affection for the house wren. Who could not love his melodious singing and playful nature? All creatures big and small play an important role in our environment. Our father instilled in us that all creatures need to be nurtured and protected, and to be free. He always made sure that they were protected and had a safe place to live during the birth of their young. My twin brother Mark and I were delighted to take part in helping our father build the bird house for his favorite bird, the house wren. The bird house was a very unique design. It was shaped like a hand and painted white. As years went by, we were responsible for taking care of the house. Interesting fact that the entrance to the house was exactly the size of a quarter. To this day, if I hold a quarter in the palm of my hand, it takes me back to a time I hold dearly. To our father and to all who cherish the natural world, we hope you enjoy this tale of one of nature's little wonders...the house wren.

—Sharon Duffield

FOREWORD

As executive producer of our *Talkin' Birds* radio show, Mark was instrumental in raising thousands of dollars in funds to launch and sustain the program and in arranging important interviews with filmmaker Ken Burns and former First Lady Laura Bush and others, and helping present the show to live audiences at the Smithsonian Institution in Washington, DC, and the Boston Museum of Science.

Mark also coordinated with the National Park Service's one hundredth anniversary celebration to bring the show to national parks like Acadia in Maine, Yosemite in California, and Grand Canyon in Arizona.

Mark also created a radio fundraising event for the Massachusetts Audubon Society at the famous Hampshire House in Boston. It's no wonder that Mark has chosen a bird subject for this richly illustrated book. It preserves the memory of his father who instilled in Mark the idea that the natural world on which birds depend must be preserved.

—*Ray Brown*

Ray Brown's *Talkin' Birds* is an interactive weekly radio show and podcast about wild birds and the natural world. Each episode features expert guests, special features about birding and conservation, and chats with our resident bird feeding expert Mike O'Connor from Cape Cod's famous Bird Watcher's General Store. *Talkin' Birds* is live streamed every week, airs on seventeen radio stations in New England and New York, and is available through most podcast providers. The show receives regular audience feedback from every US state, seven Canadian provinces, and thirteen other countries.

Find out more about the show at Talkinbirds.com and on Facebook, Twitter, and Instagram.

PREFACE

On November 20, 1905, my dad, James E. Duffield, Jr., was born in Alton, Illinois, near the banks of the Mississippi River. He would forever be known as Ted, as Theodore "Teddy" Roosevelt was president at the time of his birth, and his mother, Ma-Ma-Ma, loved the nickname.

Throughout his life, nature and birds were his passion. His father, Pa-Pa-Pa, always supported the interests of his children in what they had leanings for. He built a large chicken and pigeon coop for Dad's fourteen chickens and three pigeons. The chickens were half Brahmas and half Rhode Island Reds, and the pigeons were a Red Carnos, a White King, and a Tumbler.

My dad's other passion was building birdhouses for songbirds. Over time, as he grew older, chickens and pigeons would fly the proverbial coop, but the making of birdhouses would remain a hobby throughout his life. One bird in particular struck his fancy: the house wren. He built a special, one-of-a-kind house for his wren.

Boston, MA
November 20, 2006

AS I RECALL, on November 20, 2006, I was up early and off to work. I served as co-owner with Jennifer Hill at Blackstones of Beacon Hill, a small gift shop on Charles Street. I could walk to work in less than five minutes from my apartment on Pinckney Street. It was a beautiful fall day. The trees lining the brick sidewalks of the street were aflame with the colors of the season. The cloudless sky was that beautiful color of blue that even poets have difficulty describing. The air was cool, crisp, and invigorating.

I had a lot on my mind as I walked to work. I had only been a part of the store for six months. The store had been a beloved and successful fixture in the neighborhood for over twenty-five years. The previous owner had been an immensely popular and respected figure. She had handpicked me to be her successor. Fear of failure and of not measuring up was always in the back of my mind. A part of me wondered if I was up to the task. Previously, I had been a commercial fisherman on Nantucket Island and a fundraiser at WGBH Channel 2.

Running a store, however, was different. It required twelve-hour days, seven days a week. I had also taken on the added task of helping my friend Ray Brown establish and raise funds for his new radio show, Talking Birds, and I was on the north side of fifty! Constant worries, yes! But on this particular day, November 20, my mind drifted and was lifted with thoughts of my father. If he were still alive today, he would be celebrating his 101st birthday. I wished him a silent happy birthday and wished he were here to counsel me as in days of yore. In a way, of course, he always shared my walk.

I arrived at the store and unlocked the door. It was 8:30 in the morning. When I entered, I felt something brush my ear. I swatted at it. It was not unusual this time of year to have those large blue-bottle flies buzzing about. I thought nothing more of it. I hung up my yellow slicker and went down-stairs to the basement to price Christmas inventory. We didn't open until 10:00 a.m.

At 9:00 a.m., I could hear someone pounding on the door upstairs. I went up to find my friend Karen. She was hoping she could come in early to buy a birthday card she needed. Absolutely. While exchanging pleasantries, she quieted for a second.

"Do you hear that?" she said. I did. It was a chirping sound. A familiar sound I had heard before.

We searched all over the store to locate the source of the sound. In a short time, Karen discovered a small bird sitting in a Nantucket Lightship napkin holder, a small bird with a song I knew well. It was a wren! My dad's favorite bird. What are the odds? On what would have been my dad's 101st birthday, his favorite bird flies in with me.

The wren sat motionless in the napkin holder. He didn't budge at all when I picked him up in the palms of my hands. As best as I could gather, the wren had flown in with me when I entered the store. While I was downstairs, he most likely tried to fly out through the clear picture window and knocked himself senseless.

I really wasn't sure what to do with him. I thought at first to place him in the flower box we had outside until he regained his strength to fly away, but there were cats in the neighborhood, so I thought better of it. We had a round merchandise table in the front of the store that was positioned several feet from the front door. On the table was a top hat turned upside down that we used as a prop. Perfect! I placed the wren in the hat and opened the door. My hope was that when he regained his strength he could hop onto the lid of the hat, survey his surroundings, and fly out the door to freedom.

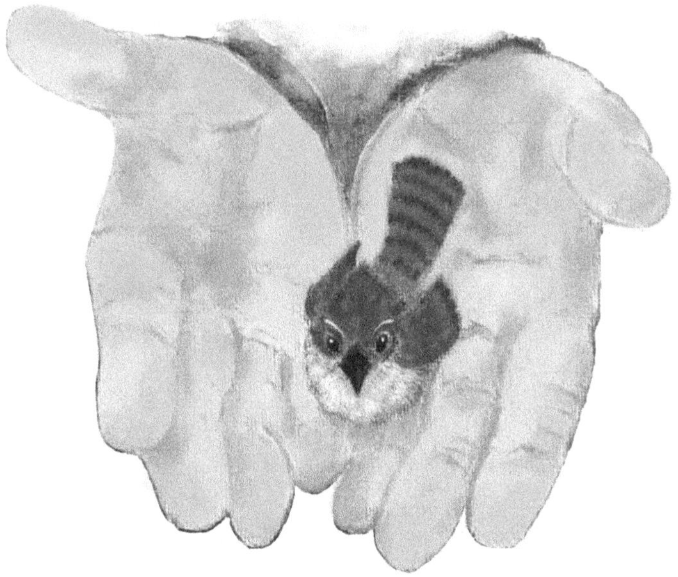

The wren is a beautiful looking little bird with a song that's just as beautiful to hear. They are small and compact with a flat head, short wings, and a fairly long, slightly hooked beak. Wrens are brownish in color with a light grey breast and have a long tail that is often erect and lifted above the body line. I never understood why Dad loved the wren above others, but there was no mistaking the care and creativity he put into building and providing a safe home designed specifically for the wren and no other bird—a special home he placed in the small backyard of our home in Connecticut.

As we awaited the wren's recovery and return to flight, my mind traveled back in time to our home in southern Connecticut—our home for forty-five years. My dad designed and built the wren house from within a small workshop in the back of our garage. Our little backyard was ringed with colorful flower gardens and a cluster of tall trees. It was a tiny but magical area and home to butterflies, bumblebees, ladybugs, and an occasional praying mantis—a perfect setting for a wren house. Dad selected a location in the center of the rear of the yard that could be viewed from the kitchen window. My mom was delighted that she would have a bird's-eye view!

The birdhouse my dad designed for the wren was very unique. The face of the wren house was a hand. Do you remember the old expression that a bird in the hand is worth two in the bush? The actual house for the wren was positioned behind the hand. It was a square box with a slanted roof with a tar shingle on top. The entrance to the birdhouse was a hole about the size of a quarter. There was no perch attached. The whole house was painted white. It would be positioned on a post. There were reasons for all of this. Dad had done his research. He brought to his task decades of experience, dating back to those early days on the Mississippi River.

Wrens usually don't like houses that sway in the wind. Stability is the name of the game, so the proper positioning of a wren house is on a post six to ten feet tall. The roof of the wren house should be slightly slanted towards the rear so that it sheds water to keep the nest cozy and dry. Dad added the tar shingle on top for added protection so that no water would leak in. The wren would be snug as a bug in a rug.

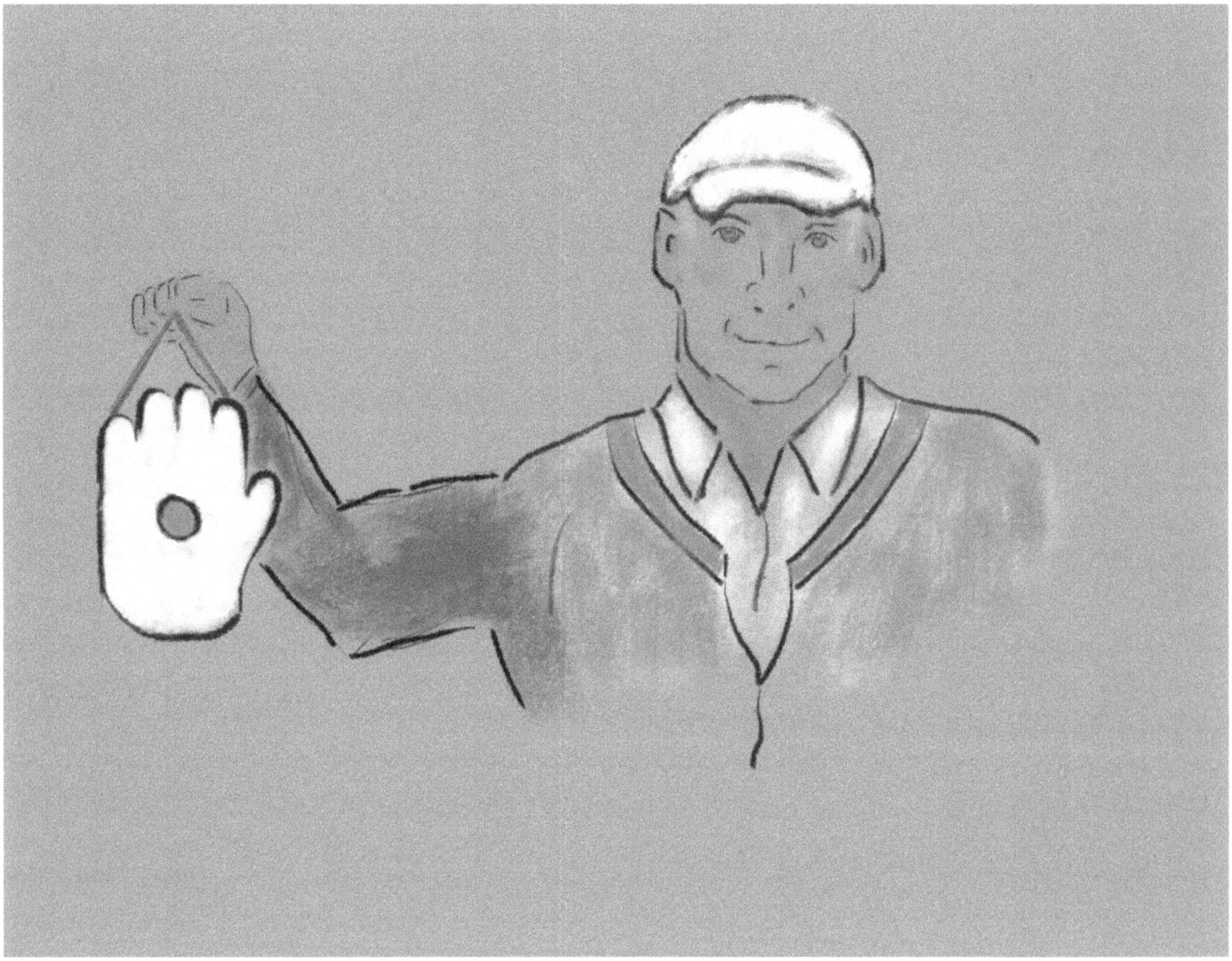

The reason for not having a perch was important because adding one would give other nosy birds an easier access to the wren's private quarters. The hole, or entrance, to the wren house was designed on the same general idea—to keep intruders out. The hole was roughly the size of a quarter. If it were any larger, other birds, like the house sparrow, could pay an unwanted visit. The floor of the house inside was also small. It was only about four or five inches square, but it provided plenty of room for the wren and the usual clutch of five or six small eggs. The wren house was painted white so that Mom could easily spot it.

Dad's wren house was a marvel of design and a thing of beauty, but like any house, it needed constant maintenance and repairs, a new paint job, and sometimes a complete do-over. That is where my twin sister, Sharon, and I came in. Over the years, my father built, repaired, and rebuilt this birdhouse many times. In his workshop, Sharon and I would help. Sharon loved to draw the circle around the quarter for drilling later on. I slapped on a coat of white paint, probably mostly on myself! Every season, we would take turns cleaning the inside, being careful not to disturb the nest, as many wrens will re-nest if everything is neat and tidy.

As Sharon and I worked on the wren house, Dad would entertain us with stories. He was a natural-born storyteller. Spending all his summers on the Duffield farm in Keosauqua, Iowa, he was among many storytellers. I think his love of storytelling and his love of birds collided on the front porch of the old farmhouse at sundown.

After a long day's hard work milking cows and pitching hay, the family gathered there, and the nightly story hour commenced. Aunt Nellie, Cousin Ed, Ma-Ma-Ma and Pa-Pa-Pa, Edith and Shorty, and others joined my dad on the porch, where they would sit passing down oral history and spinning yarns. Then, Dad would say, as he wrote in his memoirs, "Like a whisper in the night, we would hear the call of the whippoorwill. A precious moment, a precious memory."

One story he loved to tell was an old European folktale—how the wren became the king of the birds. It went something like this:

A meeting of all birds gathered to compete in a contest to see who would be crowned the king of birds. The title would be bestowed on the bird who flew the highest. All birds big and small entered. The smaller birds fell by the wayside as they tired easily. As expected, the mighty eagle soared higher than them all. The eagle only tired when he had flown higher than any other bird. A sure winner, he turned in triumph towards earth to claim the title of the king of birds, But, hidden in his large wings was a wren who flew out and flew higher in the sky and returned to become the king of birds. From then on, the wren would enjoy the reputation for energy, wit, and cleverness.

Coincidentally, I thought, these were qualities my dad shared. Dad also shared the many myths surrounding the wren. For instance, what does it mean when a wren or any bird flies into your house? Well, it foretells that an important message will soon follow. However, if the bird dies or is white, this foretells death. Killing a wren would bring bad luck to anyone. My dad always added that killing any living creature would bring ruin to any human soul.

Dad reminded us that the wren brings the promise of good fortune. They are happy social birds and love to sing. And with all its energy and enthusiasm, the wren is a symbol of joyous life and a reminder that we should strive for the same happy-go-lucky nature and to bestow kindness onto others.

I guess the thing I remember most about Dad's birdhouse is the distinctive carved hand that held in its palm a safe home for the wren. A bird in the hand is worth two in the bush—that is to say, it is better to hold onto something one has already than to risk losing it by trying to attain something better. I'm told that it is written in the Bible—don't ask me where—that God has engraved our names on the palm of His hand so that he never forgets us.

In a way, I guess it's the same for the wren. As he sits in the palm of Dad's birdhouse, I believe he will never forget the name of Ted Duffield. For Sharon, my siblings, and me, the story of Dad's wren house has always been a symbol in this way. The love and care that Dad dedicated to providing a safe refuge for the wren was the same love and care he provided for all of us.

Back in the store, an hour or so passed. Many customers came in and marveled at the sight of the wonderful songbird. It is amazing how people are drawn to the wonders of nature.

After a while, we watched as our wren regained his strength. He hopped up on the lid of the top hat, gazed around a bit, and slowly turned his head towards us. I like to think he was looking directly at me. To the delight of all, he then sang a little song, paused for a moment, and quietly sailed out the door. He flew away and soared way up into the blue autumn sky. Higher and higher. Higher than an eagle. Higher with a determined purpose he flew. It wasn't hard to imagine who he was flying to meet.

One of our customers turned to thank me for the experience and said, “If you treat your customers in the same kind manner as you have this little bird, you will be here for a long time.”

In folklore, wrens were believed to be a link between this world and the next, and on November 20, 2006—the day that my dad would’ve turned 101 years old—I, for one, don’t doubt this for a minute! No, sir! Not me!

Now the wren has gone to roost

and the sky is turning gold.

Turning from the past, at last

And all I've left behind.

—Ray LaMontagne

Happy Birthday, Dad!

COMING SOON:

AS I RECALL...
THE EXPLORER
7
WRITTEN BY MARK DUFFIELD
ILLUSTRATED BY NANCY O'HEARN

MARK DUFFIELD is a former commercial fisherman from Nantucket Island, a small business owner, and a world traveler who found his way to WGBH-TV and Radio in Boston. This unusual background provided the inspiration for many of Mark's stories. He has self- published two books, AS I RECALL: Fireflies in the Night and THE LAST SHEPARD and Tales of the Tenth Ornament: A Wee Yarn of Wonder at Christmastime.

NANCY O'HEARN is a self-taught illustrator. She was inspired by her talented mother who illustrated magazine ads during World War Two. Nancy recently retired as a Post Office letter carrier. She is now grateful to be able to fully pursue her lifelong love of art and working with dogs.

Review Requested:

We'd like to know if you enjoyed the book. Please consider leaving a review on the platform from which you purchased the book.

Lightning Source UK Ltd.
Milton Keynes UK
UKHW050341150223
416696UK00011B/297

9 781682 357248